Under the Legislature of Stars

Under the Legislature of Stars

62 New Hampshire Poets

Edited by
Rick Agran
Hildred Crill
Mark DeCarteret

With an Introduction by
Maxine Kumin

OYSTER RIVER PRESS

 For a full list of permissions and acknowledgments, see page 94.

ISBN 1 882291-59 x

Book design by Tom Allen, Pear Graphic Design
Cover photograph by Philip Scalia, Philip Scalia Photography, Exeter, NH

First Printing 1999
9 8 7 6 5 4 3 2

Oyster River Press, 20 Riverview Road, Durham, NH 03824
603-868-5006

Acknowledgments

We wish to thank the many people who helped us on this project, to whom we are greatly indebted. Thanks in particular to: Tom Allen of Pear Graphic Design; Philip Scalia Photography, Exeter, NH; the staff of the Poetry Room at the Lamont Library, Harvard University; Ed Carpenter; Josephine N. Hughes and Mimi White, editorial advisors and proofreaders.

Contents

Editors' Foreword

New Hampshire has exhibited a fiercely original, ingenuous, and yes ingenious behavior long considered integral to any endeavor, even poetry. Scratch off just a little of its conservative coating and you'll discover a literary legacy as distinct and superlative as anyone's, even when compared with its tradition-steeped, laurel-laced New England neighbors, especially given its size. Cummings, Frost, Sarah Josepha Hale ("Mary's Lamb"), Hall, Kenyon, Kumin, Nash, Simic, Thaxter (who was visited on the Isle of Shoals by Emerson, Thoreau and Hawthorne, among others), as well as Robert Lowell, who is buried here along with Cummings, Ogden Nash and the novelist Willa Cather, have all graced and sometimes cursed the state for its quirks and its orneriness. But this, more often than not, makes for a poetry that's written for its own sake, beaten out of both solitude and the bushes.

The possibilities of demographics aside, what better whereabouts to gauge the state of poetry as we enter a new century. After all, they still trust us with the first primary. Having seen New England anthologies bogged down with rusty-toothed narratives and tea-tarnished leaflets, we attempted to uphold our age-old practice of resisting too much governing and of always erring towards freedom by assembling a collection which is more of an exchange or a meeting place, rather than a who's who or a canon of some sort. Here's a gathering of poems that's in progress, always working to get there. A Yankee concoction, one part method, two parts risk, unwilling to proselytize or dispense too much wisdom, which is sometimes our way. But as anyone who's spent time here knows, locals usually have one foot planted while the other one dangles from the granite cliff airing out its toes.

For nothing is written in stone, even for those who've been here since birth. Just peruse a New Hampshire map and chance on the town of Starr King or Slab City, Sandwich Landing, Plan, Severance, Freedom or East Unity. For editors, these discoveries seem a challenge to uncover more. What once seemed familiar now brims with surprise and opportunity. So we looked for poetry which responded to the question of what is possible with as open and wide a range as we could, exploring the tensions and connections inherent in our society (both fences and bridges make good neighbors) without offering the quick-fix, easy-mix of most other mediums. Although we consciously steered away from excessively overt New Hampshire icons such as Maple Syrup and the Old Man of the Mountain, we were intrigued by the likelihood that something of the geology, flora, fauna and anthropology would emerge. And it did in extraordinary ways: snow, mud season, town meetings, foreclosures, attics, barns, bears and beech trees, ice fishing, thistle and sweet grass, riverbanks, a stone boat. But we were also taken to places as distant as Brazil and the Philippines.

As both poets and editors, we brought our own divergences to the selection process, differences on style and form, on ideas about what poetry is, does and should do when it's presumably our common language, the love of which pulled us together in the first place. We aimed for a variety of voices that shared in a sense of daring and uniqueness, as well as a demonstration that the poets took their discipline seriously. Quality, in the end (though God knows a little humor didn't hurt), was our final criterion. But it's best for us to move aside and let these poems speak for themselves. The sequence in which they appear was determined by using a random number generator to assign a value between 0 and 1 to each poem. Then they were put into ascending numerical order. The poems, whether reluctant or jubilant, implausible or celebratory, we bring out into the open, these singular voices together into this assembly—"singing, not to sing" like Frost's inimitable ovenbird.

Rick Agran
Hildred Crill
Mark DeCarteret

Introduction

In our lightly populated state, famous for its proliferation of moose and black bear, there also exists a thriving indigenous species—the poet. Unlike the moose and bear, which run true to form from generation to generation, the New Hampshire poet exhibits rich diversity.

To survive in any landscape, the poet needs to be sturdy and independent; the New Hampshire poet is no exception. His and her subject matter ranges widely, from a foreground dotted with "meadow-rue and hoary alyssum" to the wryly noted "good oak" and "killer frost." The horse-pull and the ox-pull are both present, though neither Marie Harris nor Mark Webster expresses dismay at the harsh nature of this sport. For a violent electrical storm, read Alice Fogel; for a catalog poem that wrenches the heart, there's Kate Gleason's foreclosure sale. A self-destructive teenager erupts in a poem by Cleopatra Mathis, and Mekeel McBride sketches a troubled drunk in a snowstorm. A Filipina washerwoman is the subject of Catherine O'Brian's closely textured portrait; a dismembered starfish, the subject of Julia Older's thoughtful "Beached."

Jennifer White writes about a couple at a nudist camp, photographed by Diane Arbus. L. R. Berger has a portrait of a carpenter's small son, already deeply imbued with Christian fundamentalism, and Lisa Bourbeau contributes a prose poem about a concentration camp. Stephen Dignazio is represented with a shaped poem suggestive of a butterfly, but it's a *boustrophedon*, which will send the attentive reader to his/her dictionary. And, wonder of wonders, thanks to Robert Dunn, there's a real sonnet in this anthology, a rare find these days of ever freer and more experimental verse.

Something lies in wait here for everyone, which is the true purpose of an anthology, "a miscellany, an assortment, or a catalog, as of complaints, comments, or ideas." Poems can be any or all of these. The word itself derives from the Greek for a gathering of flowers. But don't think hothouse alone, or roses or lilies. You will find thistles within as well, and bindweed, and even the rebarbative sting of nettle, which is as it should be.

MAXINE KUMIN

Poems

William Doreski

September Baptismal

Elegance of swallows and cats:
everything that flocks or crawls
seems innocent as clothes on the line.
Of course I'm tired of Wordsworth,
but note how buttery the sun looks,
how beetles make lace of my beans.
Though I'm subtle as a dishrag
still I sometimes ache to describe
the visceral fire of a mouse
or the iron fangs of a violet.
Elegance: all nature's the color
of cigars, but modest as cement.
Note how the city of Boston grows
with a vegetable persistence:
even cancer's a form of life.
We thrive on it, found in beef,
in additives, in clumsy verse.
But who needs it when good oak falls
and ruffles the landscape in love
and temper, when the killer frost
hasn't heard it's named for a poet?

■ Jennifer White

A Husband and Wife in the Woods at a Nudist Camp, N.J. 1963

—On a Photograph by Diane Arbus—

I like to look at her imperfections:
the droopy shoulders, the lop-sided breasts,
and on her abdomen, the inflections
of a scar that ends just above the nest

of her pubic hair. Mostly, her wide hips
are the magnet to which my eyes return,
partly because of her head and her flip-
flopped feet that seem so small. A misshapen urn.

A child's top. Even her gaze is askew.
He, on the other hand, is the picture
of symmetry: his eyes look straight into
mine through the camera's narrow aperture;

his nose, navel, prick form a *y*-axis
on the Cartesian graph of his body.
I could chart the coordinates of his
nipples easily, despite my shoddy

math skills. Does she, I wonder, flesh them out
with her mouth, or is she as demure as
she appears? Maybe he shows her the route
to trace. Maybe she suckles like she is

his baby. He is so clearly her guide.
Their nudity allows me to leap right
to their sex life: they have no place to hide,
there are no fig leaves around (he holds bright

car keys in his hand, but they are too small,
too cold). Besides, they joined the colony
to be free, to recapture a pre-Fall
mood. God. She seems so different from me.

She might be the perfect, the intended,
Eve. Who would refuse, dry-mouthed, pure, to slake
her thirst with fruit. No matter how red.
Who would, with certainty, turn from the snake.

I know this: I would have to stare, eyes big,
without power or desire to restrain
myself. The thick muscle moving over twigs,
through grass. Hypnotic green of shifting skin

and scales. Eyes like amber with onyx slits.
Forked tongue caressing soft *S*-sounds. All for
me. So beautiful, this serpent, and yet,
so evil. How to resist, to ignore

the flirtation, the parched throat? The tension,
like sweet meat, between awe and revulsion?

■ Charles W. Pratt

Brass Rubbing

We touched the hidden forms
As gently as a lover could,
Then took the wax and rubbed
Until a knight and lady stood
Revealed, like breath on glass;
And now, benign and timeless, they
Are watching from a frame
The mingled pressures of our lives:
What we, when rubbed, become.

James Rioux

Janitor

In the evenings the hallways grow longer
And the dust hums down from the rows
Of fluorescents. The chalk-dry air's dull singe
Still brings memories: the white stub
Clicking across slate, the cramped desks
And fidgety creak of swiveled chairs,
The hands flung wild into the air. . . .

My bones don't fit right anymore. I hear
The milling in the hip's socket
As I shuffle over the worn black tile,
The day's waste gathered to a wide dry mop,
Shaken out into a pile, the sound
Like an old dog rising from a nap.
After the first sweep I spray down the oil
And pass the clean mop's soft shag belly
Over the drizzled floor. Before me
The shimmer. Behind me the shine.

■ Matt Jasper

Rorschach Test

I call this green ink blot
in the shape of a bear
"grass bear."
*
This is an eagle
being blown apart by a bullet
or by the wind.
*
The antlers of a doe flying on a red sunset.
Her secret, right
here. It's how she makes the babies.
*
Mice playing.
It means the cat is away.
Means tiny footprints:
feet of adultery on the clean floor.
*
A dog rearing on its haunches.
He has eaten a gravy-soaked sponge.
He leaves no footprints and soon the other animals
can see only his black teeth.
*
The man on the window ledge.
*
The air is still here—
the air between the things in the room.
But the things themselves
have disappeared.
*
Like the river.
The water and a snake going up to the sky.
That's bad luck—
a snake going up to the sky for a river.

■ Mekeel McBride

The Secret Part of the Moon

All night, snow sweeps in so fast, so hard
the largest city on earth turns lunar, sifty, still.
Only our voices, like the wings of dime-store parakeets,
flutter against each other like hoped-for flight
in the miraculous absence of engines.

Down the street, a stranger, a skinny man
with stiff coppery hair pulls from a windshield
a pane of ice. "Like a Ouija board," he yells
breaking it against a parking meter before his hand
can soften it into news of the future.

It's three a.m. Drunk, he calls for someone, anyone
to make a path. "*To where?*" you whisper. The streets,
usually littered with bullet casings, are as clean as the sleep
of St. Augustine. You are not touching me in a way
that anyone can see. The snow keeps falling.

"*Let this last a little while longer, just as it is,*" you whisper,
gazing across the clean expanse before us, "*so I can love
the moon, the full moon, especially the secret part of it
I made myself.*" Underneath the burial ground
of the century's last great storm,

the sea smooths into place at the warmest edge
of its vast green territories, a bed where we might,
at last, lie down together. Perhaps something like this.
Who is still awake with us? The snow, as it continues
the soft chronicles of its own dispersal.

■ Christopher Dornin

This Guy I Share My Cell With

He's got these brown hands
from staining clocks. Sorry,
call them timepieces.

I've watched him kill an afternoon
rubbing a face smooth.
The sandpaper has a nice

sound. You can picture the ocean
or a bunch of birches with silver
leaves all twisted over.

He strokes the grain this funny
way. Reading it. Just his hand
breathes. "What's the game?"

I ask, "Limbs or trunks?"
He taps a sounding board,
"I'm just a carpenter," he says.

This mound of pink dust
grows beside his right arm
like a brand new grave.

We wake in his dust. We breathe it.
If you lit a smoke the whole
place would blow up.

All these perfect hands
twitch like wings when his twelve
grandfathers toll noon.

■ Marie Harris

The Seventh Day

Up the road from the Town Dump, this side of the ballfield, the sand pit is an arena defined by snow fence sagging in the heat where neighbors made strangers by a long winter drink beer, wait for the annual horse pull to begin. Today there will be no clearing of pine stands, no emptying fields of rock, no hauling of hay. Today, as if in deference to the commandment, paired and harnessed in Sunday leather and brass, they will pull and pull a stone boat to no practical end. Two men will gallop behind them with the hitch. One man will drive them. He will shout like a preacher *Back! Back! Back!* until they become at a crucial instant one gathered muscle, one heart, one astounding, weightless lunge. And they could pull, on a fulcrum of hoof, the weight of the world.

■ Maxine Kumin

Shelling Jacobs Cattle Beans

All summer
they grew unseen
in the corn patch
planted to climb on Silver Queen
Butter and Sugar
compete with witch
grass and lamb's-quarters
only to stand naked, old crones,
Mayan, Macedonian
sticks of antiquity
drying alone
after the corn is taken.

I, whose ancestors
put on sackcloth and ashes
for the destruction of the Temple
sit winnowing the beans
on Rosh Hashonah
in the September sun
of New Hampshire.
Each its own example:
a rare bird's egg
cranberry- or blood-flecked
as cool in the hand
as a beach stone
no two exactly alike
yet close as snowflakes.
Each pops out of the dry
husk, the oblong shaft
that held it,
every compartment a tight fit.

I sit on the front stoop
a romantic, thinking
what a centerpiece!
not, what a soup!
layering beans into
their storage jars.
At Pompeii the food
ossified on the table
under strata of ash.
Before that, the Hebrews
stacked bricks
under the Egyptian lash.

Today
in the slums of Lebanon
Semite is set against Semite
with Old Testament fervor.
Bombs go off in Paris,
Damascus, New York,
a network of retaliations.
Where is the God of
my fathers, that I

may pluck Him out of the lineup?
That I may hand back my ticket?

In case we outlast
the winter, in case
when the end comes
ending all matter,
the least gravel
of Jacobs Cattle remain,
let me shell out the lot.
Let me put my faith in the bean.

■ James Washington Jr.

Fuse Box

When he blew
the first time,
his hand was empty.
She swallowed an eyetooth,
sipped a nightcap
of salt and blood.

At sunrise
she apologized,
filled his fist
with their luckiest penny
and powdered the blues
at a wincing mirror.

■ James Duffy

Prayer

The fisherman stands on the lake
by his fire. There is water
in the trees.

I cannot
stop watching the unblinking
eye of the broken bird.

My mother's wet hands on my shoulder.
My father, the razor,
small blood on his face.

Flames of gathered grave markers:
Reflected in the sniper's eye,
a child rocking on her sled.

I push my mouth through frost,
a little church
beneath my breathing.

■ Sidney Hall, Jr.

Field Song

Who pulled out the weeds between the stars?
Who scratched the blackness and planted it?

Was it the half-wit boy
I saw this morning,
Chewing a blade of grass in a field full of
Asters?

Or was it his older sister,
Who brought him a sandwich
In a hand-made basket?

Was it his kind brother,
Who came with a book and tried to teach him to add
Two and two?

Or was it his father,
Who came by and put
A stone in his heart?

Or was it his beautiful mother,
Who came by and saw

The uneaten sandwich,
The unread book,
And the unused stone,

And ran her long fingers through his blond hair,
And smiled at him, and left?

Hildred Crill

His Future

Minuscule feats of India ink
under the whisker of a crow quill:
someone's name on a rice grain,
or a letter so small it's the postal
landscape in a blink, its postmark
an intricate speck, its destination
larger than anyone imagines.

Square one of origami,
it's a flat house, walled
with tabula rasa, quarters
too cramped for sleepwalking,
too recent for haunting,
no garden for grazing, a realm
without earshot for echoes.

A perfect bonsai of experience,
the letter writer sees
what his hand has done.
The inside of the envelope
grows into a slogan, a future
acre on billboard. The gesture
of design gallops into
his signature—waiting
for rich grass to grow,
a miniature horse of the Eocene.

■ Richard W. Moore

The Gift

A beech tree holds the prints
of bear claws in its skin
where a she-bear, years ago,
climbed to a crotch and settled in,
breaking and gathering limbs
and feasting on the beechnuts.
I led you to them last year.
Now you are showing them
to everyone.

■ Robert Dunn

In your absence I have written your name—
Lacking your face, the darkness where you sleep,
Fearing the empty darkness without shame—
And these two words the talisman I keep.
There is your name upon an envelope;
A pencil and a letter sheet have mine—
Words are a hayrake and you cannot hope
To have the wisps that slip around each tine.
What can you harvest in this barren place;
Can reaping words have scope to move here long?
But words can move within a narrow space;
And their concordant moving makes a song
In your name, which I find enough to say
Truly to pipe the one tune I can play.

■ Patricia Fargnoli

Watching Light in The Field

It may be part water, part animal—
the light—the long flowing whole
of it, river-like, almost feline,
shedding night, moving silent
and inscrutable into the early morning,
drifting into the low fields,
gathering fullness, attaching itself
to thistle and sweetgrass,
the towering border trees,
inheriting their green wealth—
blooming as if this
were the only rightful occupation,
rising beyond itself, stretching out
to inhabit the whole landscape.
I think of illuminations, erasures,
how light informs us, is enough
to guide us. How too much
can cause blindness. I think of memory—
what is lost to us, what we desire.
By noon, nothing is exact,
everything diffused in the glare.
What cannot be seen intensifies:
rivulet of sweat across the cheekbone,
earthworm odor of soil and growing.
The field sways with confusion
of bird call, mewlings,
soft indecipherable mumblings.
But in the late afternoon, each stalk
and blade stands out so sharp and clear
I begin to know my place among them.
By sunset as it leaves—

gold-dusting the meadow-rue and hoary alyssum,
hauling its bronze cloak across the fences,
vaulting the triple-circumference
of hills—I am no longer lonely.

■ Julia Older

Beached

> *We picked out a starfish; the moment we touched it one by one it disjointed all its sections until nothing was left of it save the little, round body—*
>
> Celia Thaxter

We are starfish in flesh
washed onto the land.
Our limbs move in circles
and surround us with visions.

With fear we remember
the touch that dismembers
the cardinal points.

Good-bye handsome armature,
right hand of David.
Good-bye underneathside of stars
that we wished on.
Good-bye now the only ray
left in the twilight.

The bright center core
is no meal for star eaters,
but, pointless as sandmoons,
how do we get back?

■ Andrew McCarter

from *Entries & Exits: A Notebook*

It's a descent while waking; rising from sleep, but keeping my eyes closed over the memory of the morning my little sister stood up in our bed, tiptoed on her pillow to reach the wooden crucifix which hung above our heads every night. She pried its tiny nails loose with her teeth and fingers, cast them on her night-table, and chucked the cross like a tomahawk. She then tucked Christ in bed between us. His sleepy eyes, thin grimace, the whittled muscles of his arms tense with a stretch meant for morning sharpen in my mind, as I wake to the punishment of having to hammer it back together, while our father measures my sister's reach to hang the whole thing slightly higher.

■ Don Wellman

Wooden Flutes

Wooden flutes of wood notes squeak
Some plastic more mellow
But rosewood
                                        wood rose
The yard my daughter plays in
                                                        plays
a game
of what it is to be
in prison
Coils of barbed wire
Saw bands, teeth like shark's teeth
like gleaming bone
I have not seen anyone
                                        walk in the yard that was a cornfield
before
I want to say it is a farm
They taught the children about animals there
                                        and on the hill a milk separator
covered with canvas
Canvas, crepe
Draped
over the shining metal
The men in woolen suits play flutes
on a summer's eve
Striped ties
Stripped tease
Wiggle like a worm
It's a game they play in Zimbabwe
A ritual
The Kingsnake descends from a branch
                                                                above the path

The path does not lead straight anywhere
It goes round and round
A searchlight erases the stars
When the baton falls
                                        crushing the skull
They call it the virgin's foot
But the light is a point
                                          like breathing quickly before
letting go
So many turn away as I do now
                                                              to look back
on the field
where I tied the animals for slaughter
A butcher and a philosopher
                                      both in one person
It sounds odd
Cold meat draws the blood from your hands
Cold steel turns your skin gray
The sweat on your brow is cold
Rooms in old houses
                                        have known deaths and fevers
Nightmares and love-makings
have transformed the walls
And truly good people have looked down from the windows
at the flowers
and considered their debts
One spring, several mornings in a row, a male oriole
                          made sorties against his reflection in the dusty glass
A black girl looked out her window and saw a man in white robes

hang from a flag pole
and flutter above the street
She thought him God
Go now
Leave
Neither tunnel nor fly
Enter the bush
Rose thorn
Thorn apple
Thrush

■ Mark W. Roberts

March 32nd Meltdown

The shadbush bleed white in the March-muddy hills.
Pails jangle under the taps on the maples.
I have coaxed a smile or two out of you
doing slushy spaniel impressions
but it's not enough.
I shall need all the intrigue of leprechauns
to prove that it's Spring.

Inhale, my love.
The breeze is sick to death of balsam
and paper mills.
Mangrove and bougainvillea revive it
with buckets of warm brine
and bouquets tossed to mandrills
by giddy Amazon brides.

The palettes in our brainstems shimmer.
To hell with the constant drizzle.
Suck a rum punch from a coconut.
Let your hair down
and I'll braid it for a buck.

Let's dream.
The acrobatics of the orioles will astound us.

We won't dabble, my love.
Our brushes will slap great primary streamers
across this grayness.

Call me Paolo.
I'll call you Georgiana.

■ Lysa James

Ana Cecilia's Invocation to Yemanjá on the Day She is to Enter the Convent

At dawn on this second day of February in the sacristy
of the Church of Conçeicão de Praia
I sit in the family pew sewing a shroud
of forgetfulness and ash, inevitable.
In the incense-burnished air a black-winged fly
buzzes aimlessly around the altar.
The priest snores in the confessional.
Another sinner weeps at the feet of a saint.
Something in this labyrinth
wishes me silent: I was born into slivers
of my mother's salted mirror, into sacrifice
by my father's razor-sharp words.
I pray for thin bamboo sticks I push slowly into my heart.
The nuns admire my pious desire.
"Father, forgive me for I have sinned."
But God's sister rises from the sea,

far across the City of All Saints. She is the one
my father banished from my bedside. But Maria,
her black skin shimmering with light and kitchen scents,
whispered Yemanjá's chants to me like lullabies—
Saravá, Saravá, Yemanjá Odo Ya—
quietly so my parents would not know.
I slipped into dreams, her lush voice in my ear.
And now I am here in these catacombs
and Maria sways amidst the faithful on the shore
sending offerings of flowers, peppered cakes,
oranges, and amulets in small boats alight with candles.
She prays for me. The sun sends blessings
from the edge of the world. Yemanjá, mother of all waters,
of the root-born spirits who warm the hollows of our bodies,
protector of those who travel dark waters,

carry me to the drums becoming the throb of blood,
drawing the spirit in—a taste of smoke on the tongue,
the scent of the earth in the skin,
the fearful rapture of surrender. Yemanjá
I want to become music,
washing from my tongue the ash of my father's teaching,
lifting from my back the weight of my mother's shame.
Let the tree I once saw on forbidden walks to the woods
in whose limbs I saw the spirits dancing,
in whose roots a hundred candles burned for you,
crack open this stone altar. I still see the spirits.
May this rosary turn to petal and vine.
May this shroud of burnt bone become sunrise
over waters where small boats float
and blessed fish swim the open sea.

*Yemanjá is a Brazilian *orixa* (deity) in the religious practices of Candomble. She is the powerful goddess of the sea and all waters. In February, a celebration asking for Yemanjá's protection during the coming year is held on the beach. She is based on the Yoruba goddess of the Abeakuta River.

■ Alison Harville

Themes on Distance

I.
Blue hollow dawn
Squeezing out the first flight.
Robins bend back
And nest farther from home.
The roof and chimneys,
Less acute against the sky,
Finitely fade.
          That the green umbrella leaves
          Might remember roots
          And yearn for soil.

II.
If I were a painter . . .
I could not find a color on canvas
          Sturdy enough
To be my fresh orange.
Ball of cool sweetness,
Thick skin falling in chunks.
Orange like it captured summer's air
          And was so very proud of it.
(Filling a cream bowl
Once my grandmother's
Found in old cabinet)
Orange like one might picture
Falling out of the pockets
          Of small children,
Giggling and bouncing down the stairs.
Filling up my eyes, my sight
Like nothing else mattered,
          At all
(But a color)

■ Colleen Connors

I Took From You

I pin red poppies to the lapels of veterans:
one by one they ghost-sail by, jingling
meagre pensions in ravelly soutache pockets,
rolling pennies for the brace-maker
my illicit grandfather used to be.

And no matter where you are, old man, I hear you,
fine-tuning the prosthetic pins of British soldiers.
I hear your dulcet hammers, and flaccid strings

for fins. Your face is my inheritance.
I wear it like a tiny banjo
—mbanza, mbanza with the long fretted neck.

Earth to Heaven: I ring your name.

Stonefish, megalith. In colossal dreams
I follow you down
Soho's seedy brothel stalls
where the prostitutes are laid
-out on fish-drying platforms
for the overworked coroner to study—
the faustian hunger of these soft-slippered wives
—my Czech grandmother in a breadline, waiting.

In this broken hospital of instruments
where the webs are laced with dust;
there's suet-ash in the lye,
and nothing left to hold or kiss . . .

I took from you.

Ralph Sneeden

Hummingbird in the Moving Van

Like a soul shot from a burning body,
she streaks from behind the stacked chairs,
past my head and the desk I'm shouldering,
to land in the branches of the mulberry,
not quite bird, but bee, or dragonfly.
And in the second before she streaks off
to work the orange funnels of the trumpet vine,
we face each other.
There is no imagined conversation.
I put no thoughts into her tiny head,
or words on her slim beak,
hypodermic, leveled at my face.
"What's wrong?" my wife shouts from the window,
packing tape screeching around her boxes.
I stand on the aluminum ramp, unable
to move, the weight of the desk bearing down.
I want to tell her nothing
is wrong, although my sneakers are slipping
and we have emptied our home again
to unload it an hour up the road.
Things could be worse.
I want to say . . .
It's going now.
Look, the lawn mower has made wine
from the fallen mulberries;
and the squirrels are hanging
by their back legs
to get the last of them.

■ Rick Agran

O of a Bowl

Sometimes, tired, she came to bed clay-freckled,
vaguely dusty and sweet-smelling.
He loved her long-fingered hands,
browned with afternoon sun, palms
clay-smoothed by the spinning bowls she made.

Each crease clay-defined, a hand-held topography
she curled into fists under her chin when first
they slept in the same bed.

When her breathing changed he would coax
her hands open and she would sigh in her sleep,
one palm soothed by cotton flannel, the other upturned.

Sometimes he would lay his head in her hands
and imagine himself the O of a bowl being molded,
sometimes she would awaken and squish his mouth
into a pucker, one-handed, and kiss him good-night
a second time.

■ Kate Gleason

After the Foreclosure Sale

After my grandfather died, and his cottage
was sold right out from under us, after the night fell
that last time in our eyes over the shirred pond shot with silver,
after the ringed loon returned, mateless, to its hollow,
and a squadron of wild geese followed, reaching
like the rough coastline of a map, into the cold beyond,
after our clothes were tied in bundles like yesterday's news,
and hangers rang and jangled their empty songs,
and mothballs rolled like bright, new planets
in our bare dresser drawers, breathing out
their icy halos of camphor, after the dark moons
of our faces no longer rose in the sky of the well,
after perennials were uprooted and divided,
after hummingbirds no longer whirred at the sweet feeder,
and the slink of cats stopped skulking in the grass,
after red newts no longer furled in whiskered moss,
and the rock that could be licked bluer went dry and dull,
after the red-checkered table cloth tethered with tacks,
after the built-in mirror with its peppered skin,
after all this no longer belonged,
after I tried to imagine someone else's hand
cradling the heft of our butter knife, pulling up a chair
to the table where I had secretly scarred my name,
spreading out the cheese of holes, the bowl of blackcaps,
the crust of bread, someone else's family
sleeping under the heavy drug of fresh air
and rising at dawn from the feather beds
to hear bacon sizzling like rain, fingerprints
of cream swirling in their coffee, after the Open House,
after the closing, after the developers
got their hands on the place and ran power
from the road, put in plumbing, after no one
any longer lugged lake water in clanking pails,

and acorns ceased to thrum the tin roof
with their slowest drums, after revamping, refinishing,
after the hand-cranked Victrola with its crotchety voice
and the *sumo*-squat, unbudgeable icebox
were budged out the door, after our wallpaper
was peeled like a deed torn between brothers,
and the next generation of fireflies stopped arguing
against the punctured heavens
of mason jars, after the graces of birches
no longer leaned and huddled like sisters,
after the guilty oaks were thinned of their shade,
and blowsy lilies drowsed in sunlight's sleep,
and Mt. Monadnock lifted the scoured god
of its peak, after the same but different fish
kissed open the seam of the lake, after the same
but different sun sent down its spokes into the deep,
and the towels of the new swimmers sprung
like bumper crops on the beach, after all this,
after I watched my grandfather's name
become nothing but a depression in stone,
saw his land and home go under
another name, saw the place rented—
groomed, vacuumed, and purified of my childhood,
saw the swarm of seasonal people
flock with their raucous radios, stake
their silly umbrellas in their clinkering drinks,
and fold their hands over their indulgences,
after all I have known of this place—the must
and pine of it, every nook that mysteried me,
every rock that skinned me—tell me,
how can I love
what is left?

■ Melanie Walsh

inventory

i'm all about wanting to be a hard shell. a mango that won't bruise. a lost passion.

i'm all about a juggling act. sore arms. a dizzy head. a couple of inhalers.

i'm all about solitude. the breath i won't give up. being my own leech. a lone body.

i'm all about a lack of sleep. a plucking freak. a gnawing mouth. an upset stomach.

i'm all about my freckled back & turning it.

Donald M. Murray

December 7, 1997

This is what you must know
when you lie down with a soldier
returned from battle: offering
the healing caress, finger tracing
the pink twisted river of skin, touching
tip of tongue to puckered wound,
listening to what he does not say,
imagining the distant geography
from where he has returned,
spreading your legs if you can
now become one, receive his seed,
heal: he has passed beyond feeling
into a coldness he had not known
was within him but became familiar,
his salvation and strength.

He found himself comrade
to his enemy, sharing duty,
the ease of weapons, perhaps
a blood joy he has not since found.

Even now, so long home
from war, he will not hear
what you have said, or will leave
your bed and you will find him
behind the garage staring
at the light before dawn
infiltrating your wood lot.

Do not speak. Step back.
Allow him his reunion,
the old flickering film, black
and gray, the flowering bouquets
of shellfire white, shadows
running, stumbling, falling,

rising to attack. Those huddled
in ambush and those surprised,
the stagger steps of the stretcher
bearers, all of them so young.

Admit you were drawn
to his chill mystery, that blank
landscape, the necessary cruelty
you imagined. How quick, how strong
he must have been. Remember you thought
he might protect you, might turn wild,
the wolf you feed but never tame.

■ Andrew Woolf

Losing Time

Hacking around wasting your life
So filled with holes you can't find your navel
Three years three minutes
Wordsworth lied about his past
Shelley was a bundle of nerves
Keats lost his way
And I will end up like these three gentlemen
State property
I can't erase my footprints
My past is a plum pudding
The future a predictable joke

■ Andrew Howe

Memoir

> *I am circling around God, around the ancient tower,*
> *and I have been circling for a thousand years.*
>
> Rainer Maria Rilke

Ah, the air used to pass through me
Until I dissolved, weaving through
Woods and distances between them.
When the wind stopped, I became the blowing.
If a dog was nearby, I became his panting.

Understand that even to gaze
Upon some distant star, one needs
Some broken ground beneath,
For gratitude can only come from despair.

And the evenings asked
Such small things from me.
When I turned to face the moon—
The injured turning towards the intact—
Could I really conceive its existence,
Or was it just another lie?

Forever, it seems, I have been
Standing here, alone.

Conceive then, what moving away
From the infinite space means,
Isolating for years, a foreigner
Amongst fantastic strangers
That today, at last,
I can call myself home.

J. Kates

Out

Everything will, you know. The bone
harp singing in the king's hall,
the cunning wound, tobacco-stained
carpeting, a telephone call,

Col. Mustard in the dining-room
with a wrench, Raskolnikov
in the existential gloom,
brothers wrestling over a pocketknife

on a slippery riverbank,
strangers stretched on their knees.
Fingering a pistol, jilted Frankie
nails Johnnie in his BVDs.

That's how it is: What we act
in private becomes the matter
of music, the marrow of related fact
in a storyteller's patter,

and nothing we can dream is left
without beforehand or afterwards
unaccounted for. When we laughed,
our laughter was broadcast by the birds,

and when you slammed the door
an old shaman in a weather-beaten tent
half the world away finished the story
and told me where you went.

■ S. Stephanie

Evening Interrupted by Dali

The wind blows through from Canada tonight,
its noise alone rocks the rhododendron
and sends its roots shrinking, as if blooming
weren't hard enough in this town that teeters
constantly on the edge of tourism.
What the wind doesn't kill here the salt will.
Color fades faster than dream in seaports
such as this one. The grayness of wood
seeps out from under the paint on houses
as though it were another dimension
we could push our hands in and walk through.
Dali was right, somewhere things are burning.
Especially those buildings gone quiet,
majestic against the skyline. At sunset
their windows burn so red, flaming giraffes
on the last strip of blue horizon.
Whenever I see these, despite the wind,
I feel that somewhere things are gathering,
that somewhere things are standing in clusters
as still as figures posing in backgrounds.
But what could we be waiting around for?
I don't believe my neighbors are listening
for those collapsed clocks to begin ticking
or pianos to pull themselves upright
and play. And when the wind blows
a building over, nothing seems to care
if we rebuild it. Nothing seems to be
in a hurry to live with us, instead
we seem to be tugging at indifference.
I don't want to think of things as figures
that wait with their chests open and empty
as wooden drawers not worth the rummaging,
not a tea bag or a scrap of paper,

not a stub of pencil left in them.
They make me feel sad—the way my lover
makes me feel when he says his face has gone
as creased and wrinkled as an old letter.
I don't know what to say so I distract him:
just listen to this Canadian wind
and look at our stubborn rhododendrons.
Centuries from now, I believe his face
will still be the carefully folded note
which everyone and everything has been
trying to pass me, trying to put in my hand.

■ Katherine Solomon

Hare

> *"I shall go into a hare."*
> From a witch's formula for transformation, quoted by Isobel Gowdie at her witchcraft trial in 1662.

The full-again moon sends too much
light, white nails clattering
on the roof, claws
of the ghost fox. I am no stranger

to lying low, my room cave-dark
behind thick drapes. But even here
I know I am not safe. The birch
beyond the window in the glare shakes

its bones to let me know. This
is a moment I shall not welcome
should it rise to rattle in a dark
corner of my death. I shall go

into a hare, scratch a depression
in the briars. I've torn the leaves
out of all my books, the soft down
from my thighs. In solitude

I'll try again to take nourishment
from the hope I've stuffed in haste
into my belly. The black cat
crouches in shadow. She hears

a rush of air and opens her eyes, two
yellow berries among the goldenrod.
The horned owl will crack her skull
and eat her brains. And who

can curse the hunger? I shall go
into a hare and when day comes to spring me
from this brambled nest, the thorns
that rake my sides will tremble

a sticky minute, the holy hounds
will sniff in vain. By then,
I shall be golden, leaping
through meadow clouds of pollen.

■ W. E. Butts

Grace

I wake, remembering it's been years
since I've lived alone.
Did I tell you, once I spent hours
listening to the solitude of snow?
Yesterday I watched death take the last
leaves from the elm branches, and thought
about the desire of rock and weed.
I drove to the harbor then, the confusion
of seabirds, children tossing breadcrumbs
into the gray winter air, and stood by the pier
looking out at endless shimmer and wave.
This is what the body so often comes to:
awkward gesture and grace. Last night
we made love, held each other and slept.
I believe the dreams we don't recall
are the reason we rise each day
as ourselves, and go on. We've been
to the burial grounds, names etched in slate,
the park and its child frozen at the fountain.
We've collected small stones and feathers
from the shore. Autumn in the flower garden,
bees have repeated your name inside my throat.
When I speak with you now, horses arrive
at the marketplace, their carriages silent.
What I have to say is no more than the rain.

■ Francis Golffing

To a Friend Who Found It Difficult to Write

When dry as grasshoppers your voice
Batters against your throat, let be.
Step to the window while it gives
On to the world's sweet average,

While all around nor yet too late
The slopes, the shaded lanes, the draws
Whisper enjoin commemorate
Varied intentions of terrain:

To watch a clean perspective scheme,
A web of lines coordinate
Knit with the circle and the swoop,
The lonely orbit of a bird,

And spreading through the valley floor
A holding on, a letting go,
Till between stress and counterstress
The restless eye is cancelled out,
The throat retrieves its level tone.

I see a tree across a road.
I see a road across a ridge.
The hawk entranced with what is there
Consumes and is consumed by air.

■ Hugh Hennedy

Above the Garden

Pressed by whom
if pressed at all
this yellow tassel
of wheat or other
grass

        hidden for
How long between pages
of the Last Puritan's
background accounts
published under
wartime conditions

This Chinese character
greenish yellow
overlay of black
and white spaces
this natural thing
become artifact

                    this
Summer day impinging
weightless on
this summer day
this flaxen story
within the son's story

Open now again
and again flat
within pages
superseding
wisdom

■ Ellen Hersh

Sweet Georgia Brown

Late afternoons before Dad came home
to hide behind the Wall Street Journal
in his stiff-backed chair,
wahs wahs of Fats Waller

came sailing up the stairwell
Rugs rolled back,
victrola at 78 rpm,
the three of us:

> *No gal made*
> *can cast a shade*
> *on Sweet Georgia Brown!*

Mother, with her spectators off,
Clarice, untying the white
Oxfords of her maid's uniform, and me,
kicking off penny loafers,

waited for the peppy refrain.
Mother would execute a snappy
Charleston, teaching me and
Clarice the arm movements,

> *Two left feet*
> *but oh how sweet*
> *is Sweet Georgia Brown.*

the knee crossovers
which the Charleston,
her breathless gasps
assured us, had only

stolen from the Black Bottom.
We'd Charleston that whole side,
copy Mother's tall, flat-chested torso
cut staccato flapper moves.

It's been said
she knocks them dead
when she comes to town.

Then Clarice would put the needle
back to the start, lead us through
the latest butt swooping, arm dipping
moves of the newest kind of boogie

fresh from the June Germa,
a Woodstock of the Forties in the south.
We went in order of age. Mom was
thirty-seven, Clarice twenty-nine and I fifteen.

They all sigh
and hope to die
when she turns them down.

so we got to my jitterbug last,
whirling each other in
wrist snappy three person
twirls over and over

I'd reset the needle,
Clarice would say Mother and I
could move it pretty well for white
girls as the record needle

Fellers she can't get
are fellers
she ain't met . . .

careened to dead center
when my father's car door slammed.
Clarice flattened out the rugs with her
feet as she boogied back to the kitchen.

I raced up to my room and the ablative absolute
but Mother, barely back in her spectators,
heading for my father at the door,
was still humming Sweet Georgia Brown.

■ Chris Volpe

Anemone

windowsash of flame

remedy

red-rimmed shiver gong

forest that shimmers still

birds in a wreath of myrtle

limning and shine

love's red watchman lured

barbaric softening

lifting to wave

vanish

miniature memory gesture

a world this way a world this way

anemone

Cleopatra Mathis

That Year

Winter nailed itself to the ground.
She was fourteen, breaking and freezing.
She'd slice another hole in her body,
not pierces but a ragged stitch
circling her arm. I couldn't stop her.
March came, the bad snow
kibbled to rot. Dog-given, hungry days
eating at her. A red slash
streaked through her chopped hair.
Everywhere she looked, the unyielding world
said *bad*, said *no*. More in bed than not,
she wanted her black room, the walls lined
with articles, the pictures of Cobain sprawled
dead in his Converse All-Stars, rabbits
tortured for eye make-up, the clubbed seal's fur.
She rubbed her own cut fingers into the evidence
hanging there: the perfect smiles, anorexic
and bulimic, the baby in the toilet, the stalker.
Outside, I turned my back
to the prevailing weather, studied
my good preparations—gardens I'd planted
in last fall's rain. The weeks would come
in the order of snowdrops, crocuses,
daffodils, tulips. I'd planted according
to every specification, the good mother
charting soil and depth and food.
I'd made them all. Everything in my rich dirt
was sure to rise.

■ Charles Simic

Needle

At ghost-hour,
Let one of your fingers
Walk the floor
Of this old house,

As if it were a
Dark forest,
With your dead mother's
Silver needle

In a bird's nest,
One lone drop of blood
Sliding down
To its sleepless eye.

■ Alice B. Fogel

Starting Small

Amidst such violence as the sky's—
with its unshielding cracks, its unwieldy enormity crashing through
and lighting up our bones—
amidst its steady, ongoing, thrumming, unrelenting forever
drumming rain, its laughing erosion of skin and lash, of wooden deck,
of river bank or garden edge, of tact—
how do the lilies,
even the little alyssum,
remain sloping upright,
neither cowed nor overturned
by such a tumbling downward
of whipping water and wind?
Or the birds unquestioning under their wings,
or the squirrels merely paused between two seeds—everything
standing to meet
the downpour, unrepentant, unafraid?
The rains rope downward,
the rains all swing
on the guffaws of air. Alight with random flashings of fire, the raining
air explodes, abstract element
transforming into sound and sense beyond
magnetic fields, electric forces, the friction of heat on frost, of clouds
on high.
In the doorway, envious at the threshold, I will myself
to lean upward into it, like a stem to enter up
into its need to plunge on down,
its utter love of release and repeat.
In fact the wild frightens me, although I choose it,
although, wet, I step onto the floating grass, catch
my hair on the dark bark
of trees that at any second
could split at the seams. I am only human
and the teeming sky—

falling hard from heaven to earth—
is too much air for me.
I want to start again, small. Tonight,
after this storm passes over,
let's heave open all the sodden windows and doors,
let's switch on the electric lights,
one for each room at least, and host
the afternoon's damp aftermath of moths and gnats,
the siren song of mosquitoes wanting only a taste
of what we hold inside, the silent tune of bat food
in search of warmth and salt: their simple greed so pure,
their fragmented plenitude like rain's abundance scattering;
let's listen to their ping and preen breezing in the halls
and pattering on lamps, the din of insects negotiating
the plausible distance from ceiling to floor—so little
they ask of us really, so little we're willing to take.

■ Lisa Bourbeau

Oswiecim

The name astonishes itself, hauled like a still warm potato up from a bed of ashes. It rasps the teeth and fills the mouth, its hidden vowels palpable, its acrid taste the worm of another tongue. It tests the sound of itself, hearing the soprano in Gorecki's third, learning itself as a prayer imprisoned, light behind stained glass, plasma.

It wants to know everything—if trees are still given permission to be trees, and all about the blanket of woolen air hung in its back yard. It wants to reclaim the shoes.

Oswiecim knows them all: the black, scuffed, worn-at-the-heel shoes, brown shoes, shoes with bows, white toeless dancing shoes, tiny thin-soled first step shoes, and that small red shoe, upside down on the top of the highest moldy mound, toe buried, from which one thin strap hangs loose, the button eyelet slightly droopy. How the shoe-filled room is parched of sound, smelling of voices whole as turned earth, shrunken to silence, to metal screaming, Oswiecim releases to the telling.

The owning, like the parting of waves, is love, radiant.

■ William Varner

Monopoly

Baltic Avenue

The old Plymouth Volaré across the street
resembles a patchwork quilt.
When the neighbor below me coughs,
I feel it in my feet.

Oriental Avenue

The steam swollen eyes of the Chinese cook
through the square window in the kitchen door
which screams like Godzilla
every time the waiters open it.
The delivery boy dancing with a broomstick
to the Taiwanese girl rock star whose voice
floats down from the speakers
like a long string of silk scarves
pulled from a hat.

Pennsylvania Railroad

The moon rushes in like a headlight
on a runaway train full of dreams.
Birds call out hidden in the sky,
the indecipherable language of flight.

Free Parking

Any empty lot
on the outskirts
of hell.

Marvin Gardens

The taxidermist and his wife
are drunk on Tanqueray and tonics,
playing croquet on the lawn.
His yellow and black bowtie,
a butterfly pinned to his shirt.

Fireworks exploding into mums of light.

Park Place

The dancing bear tattoo
on the dimpled buttocks
of the skinny little hooker
tiptoeing to see
into the jewelry store window.

landscape is quiet *writ*
now disregard with *over*
recounted in alphabetic space
it of much so
equals the time telling
ox an as dumb
in a(n) hungry wave
at dispersing it of
the edges as I
it by it by

boustrophedon

■ Peter Kidd

Awaiting the Monster's Phone Call

rehearsing the ploy
rewriting the script
keeping it fresh

cross town
they set up chairs
for the song

the kettle
whistles its
constant note

fragrant fantasies
step
frontstage

"An aviary
full of
tame birds,"

the castle in the heart speaks.

Rebecca Mays Ernest

Peacetime

Before the critical eye gauged desire
mood music went for a song and borrowed
smallcraft lined its banks dotty with Christmas
trees transfixed tinsel-toothed in suppliant
stationary but rootless retirement,
cinnamon. Wrought iron cradled the back lung;
frogs complained like lap dogs locked in closets.

Suddenly his jackknife barge split the deer
crosswise almost as if a change of mind
meant heartbreak in an audience of palms
where only two fronds clap. Reflexive strife
domestication breeds that involutes
us tonguing, nuzzling, grappling conflated
prey and offspring has not shaken our view
clean shaven to this:
                                        innocence is bliss,
denatured, stunted, planar ignorance
by whose misnomer we evacuate
aught for tighter cognizance of naught.
In a bull's eye ends the yellow brick whorl
we've backed down to stay free from the unknown
fallaciously; brunt of blurred rights and wrongs
we know too much, we knew it all along.

Our formula was ruined in the storm.
Infants would pull hair, eat lye, suck breasts dry.
So like a rash on the rate of change to
be weeping poppy blood for our native
wisdom, virtual as the horizon.
God the true martyr does not help Godself
tell disordered narratives of Eden;
as gravy over what is meet even,
ladled by lantern, soldiers' worth of glory.

■ Pat Parnell

Sheila the Hat

(to the Ballinderry Sheila, Ballinderry Castle, Co. Galway)

Sheila-na-gig, I will make myself a hat
in your image. The fabric is grey and rough,
like the stone in which you are carved
on the castle wall.
Your hands hold open your lips
so they fit snugly over my ears.
My head is a giant egg you are laying
on the last bit of a breech birth
you are pushing out of yourself.

I will wear you skiing
when the bright winter sun shines blinding
off the snow.
Your lips clutch tight,
warming me with your body heat.
You crouch over my forehead, facing
into the wind, shading my eyes.
Your hands clasp under my chin,
and your legs cross over my chest,
hugging close.
Your thick braids swing across my shoulders,
thumping,
as we tuck, twist, and turn, speeding
down the slope.

The wind of our race
flattens your breasts against your rib cage.
Your Gaelic battle cry cheers me on.
Everyone who sees you will say,
"What a great hat!"

*Sheila-na-gig is a Celtic guardian spirit who wards off evil with the power of female sexuality. She is frequently portrayed squatting in the birthing position, her hands spreading her vulva.

■ Jennifer E. Whitten

Glass Eye

from "Fetishes I Carry"

It was his. Or it wasn't. He was a liar, and made
a liar of me. Now all story
bends around light, through opaque spheres,
uncertain. Clanks, struggling
to roll loose from emptied drawers. He never
wore the eye; he wore fragrant shirts, stitches
like fine lines in a face. What kind of man
would keep such a grisly talisman, and never tell
where it came from? And what sort of woman
still stores its heft, its pupil,
pretending it can see where he has gone?

■ Esther Buffler

Lost Head

from "Dream Sequence"

The curtain bangs down,
shears it, neat.
Thump. Thump.
and
there it is again, staring.
My lost head, nerves cut,
frazzled, but no blood,
just pain.

Smiling, open-mouthed, it
jumps the orchestra pit,
rolls over worn carpet,
leaps from lap to lap.
People flee.
A spot from the balcony picks it out,
turns it to ravishing pink.
It lurches out a window,
floats among the huge falling-down
buildings. Devastation,

until that stagehand
reaches for it,
motions to it, holds it,
kisses it, takes it
backstage.

My body surges up for it again.
The ache in my groin
makes me ready
to be stuck together
just once more.

■ Hope Jordan

Ice Fishing

You walk the glare avenue of my skin,
where surface boulders beckon
like lips or nipples, warmed by sun.
You touch them before going on.
All this white
hurts your eyes,
and you are tired
of me being a frozen river.

You scrape it down to where I'm alive,
dark and moving fast.
You cast
bright hooks,
and you are more than half afraid
of what you'll catch.
Whatever you get
will only die in your air.

Someday I will soften
to a surface
your boots no longer trust.
Your hooks will turn to rust.
I will swallow all
your animals, children and machines,
and they will sleep here, dreaming dreams
out of your reach.

■ Robert Herschbach

An Epic

My liege, this is a brittle place.
Cortez, with his excellent nose
Sniffing out no scent of gold
Would surely have passed it over.
And the pink dogs pawing at tubers,
The pink-bellied dogs.

Mounting each other from boredom . . .
The sky like lacerated flesh.
We went to the creek,

Which was heaving up fish. They were
A marvel, for they had no eyes or scales,
But were rubbed into pale, indeterminate
Shape. They fell apart in my hands.
And my liege, he said: find the red root.
And six of them held me down, reached
Into my mouth. And my liege, he said:
Find the magic acorn. And he held
The penknife to the soft, pink flesh
Of my ear, and I was afraid.

And he said: do not fear, for we are all
Blessed by the golden hands of the sun.
And he held up the ear, like a moist fungus.
Look how nature has blessed us, he said.

Cortez, his face like jagged rock.
His shoes, two slabs of blackened
Meat, breaded with dust. The equation
He carries in his head, like "Country Roads." It goes

Something like this: if *x* is the modest
Wingspan of days, and *y* cramps us

Into its nook, if the bigger half
Of a wishbone equals the better part
Of mercy, if the number of stones
Weighing me down shall determine
How quickly I learn to swim,

Then what use dreaming

Of cool terraces, of bare feet
On marble? And the well-fashioned
Sandal? And the wicker chair
To act as a frame

For constantly shifting thighs
And bellies, intertwining laughter?
Sticky as a damp sheet was the air.
The moon like a huge vitamin,
Undissolved

In the night's throat.
My long hair like a curtain.
He opened it, and my face
Was bald in the halflight,
A lump of white putty.

His fingers pulled back
The sleek cords, in his hands
My head was a rounded globe
On which he traced cities,
Canals. Do not fear, he said,
We are all

Already absolved, even now
Somebody's clammy fingers
Are sponging the page . . .

Mark DeCarteret

Bernadette, the Saint

In stages I have waned against the backdrop of hill,
    the wind-stiffened trees,
while my nerve endings shrank from the soundtrack
of locust, their plotting antennae, diabolical knees
summoning my blood, the spurred cells of compulsion
    to attack.

Why is it the anointed, the blessed, are always ill?
Our bodies uncaressed, the destination of no kiss
but a trembling Spirit's which sucks free the will,
arousing more of the self with each puncture,
    each escaping hiss.

Out in the distance, I am the only one made
    to be taking in the meadows
all stricken with blossoms, small children, faces taut
with oxygen and the town square beyond
    ecstatic with wheelchairs, robust shadows,
filling bottles from the springs
    with miracles they've bought.

And the whole time I'm resisting.
    While the town feasts and plays
I eat grass and grow weaker, more selfish—
    too frail now but to praise.

■ Mimi White

The Quiet

No one time can claim its hollow center.

I fall into it and risk
my name and history.

All is equal in the new air:
The open book unraveling

its tale that *will* end,
the nest of cedar waxwings

knitted to a broad branch,
the wind knocking the yellow leaves.

Time will tell is not true.
The birch trees weaken;

this is their future.
The quiet passes between their weighted boughs.

When I shut my eyes
a boat sails to its final destination.

The heroine leans against the rail
and taps her fingers

along its cold edge.
When I lift the book

it has the weight of feathers.
I cannot pick up my life

where it left off.

■ Jane Kenyon and Donald Hall

Words for a Warrant

When the stream by the Town Hall rushes
with meltwater, and early sap drips
into buckets until dusk; when the dirt back
roads thaw by noon and freeze again at night,
Bob looks for his gavel, and townswomen
tuck the town warrant into knitting baskets.
At seven o'clock on the second Tuesday in March
we enter the warm room, with its loved
and extremely uncomfortable benches, and settle
to the business of governing ourselves. Once a year,
for a couple of hours, we are civil and deliberate.
Then we stand stretching, happy
to go home, and step out into the clear,
cold night, under the legislature of stars.

■ L. R. Berger

The Carpenter's Son

When the carpenter's six-year-old son Uriah
picks out a music box from a carton in my attic,

I tell him it's broken.

He opens the lid, winding the already overworked key,
and the minuet I haven't heard for twenty years
plucks its tinpan song.

I'm a Christian, he says, as if by way of explanation.

The word broken means nothing to him.

God's in your music box, he pronounces
as we climb down complaining stairs,

and trails me out, cupping it like a nestling
he sets down inside the garden. He watches me untangle
then carefully stake each heavy, pungent vine.

God's in your tomato plants,
he says. Still, I break some.

Then he draws through his believing fingers
the tail of every blue-grained ribbon
I spliced and knotted around the fence

for discouraging birds. The word discourage
means nothing to birds.

You know, he says, *God's in your ribbons.*

■ Jeff Friedman

J, the Chronicler

After the interrogations,
after the tortures,
after the streets were chalked
with the outlines of bodies

and the lines intersected,
crisscrossed
until they formed
yellow and white

constellations—
a broken Orion,
his trunk lopped
from his muscular legs,

the big dipper
pouring out particulate,
the twins grappling
twisting each other

to the point
where sinew snaps—
after the explosions
were cut off

from our hearing
and the small country
of our desire
burst into a beautiful

soundless blaze,
gold sparks
shooting from the blue
petals of flame,

after the last herd
of extinct animals
plunged into the fire
and only ashes swirled

from the ashes, I,
who knew nothing
of government or history,
who earned my living

at a small desk
under the humming
white tubes,
created a god

out of words and paper,
a god swooping
down from the clouds,
a whistle in flight

a god whose wings
spread open
like a Chinese fan—
huddled outside

under the dark sun,
those who could
no longer read
prayed,

and someone
with a spoon
and a wooden bowl
beat out a song.

■ Rodger Martin

On the Making of Monica's Poem

"This poem is already in my head,"
and she carefully prepared its bed,
creasing each small rectangle of rice paper.
Nail polish burnished olive for cover,
For spine, a swizzle straw in perfect time.

The background thumped, the background danced
grinding up the thighs of the world
note after note after note.
Aeronautical genes align the wings of the pages,
while the artist reserves the colors
and the poem stays hidden in the end.

Paper always blossoms first
then comes the script—hard, quick, good
its pieces like fragmented scrolls
that tease us with clues.
But mystery builds like fractures
And I walk alone on the crevices.

■ Jean Pedrick

Simples

A simple against sadness
In great cities:
Go to the museum. Ask
For John Constable.

Simple for sense of loss
In vanishing country:
Drive in the rain till you
Find an old barn. Stand
In its lee, lay your cheek
On the silk of its skin.
Breathe in the dust, tin,
Leather, dung, sweet clover,
Feathers of old barns in rain.

■ Catherine O'Brian

Pasing

Pasing, our lavandera,
never smiled. Still,
my mother likes to tell me,
Pasing had a wonderful life.

But I always wondered
why Pasing never married,
why she smoked a cigar all day long,
chewed it, pressing the hot dark roll of tobacco
upon her bottom lip.

I used to watch her wash,
iron, sweep, smoke,
and balance the cigar,
watched the ashes tremble
and fall onto my mother's silk slips.
Pasing would spit on the iron, frown,
and brush the ashes away, rub the leftover
ashes into the cloth with her thumb.
Smoke darkened the windowless room,
the stub's small burn of light glowed
like a filling between her yellow teeth.

I wondered what she thought of as she stared
for hours at the crucifix on the laundry room wall,
or the picture of baby Jesus in Mary's lap,
surrounded by bluebirds, angels and lambs so white
they looked like they'd been soaked for days in bleach.

I hunched in the corner, kept away from her feet,
counted cockroaches crawling across
the gray cement walls, hoping to hear her
gossip with the gardener or tell crude stories
about the Quiapo Market's beggars and thieves.

Then she would mutter old and Asian warnings
under her breath. I watched her eyes.
And sometimes, breathing a sigh of hot, foul smoke,
Pasing would sit down on her cot, remove her slippers,
remove her sweaty dress, slowly rub each foot with cocoa butter,
half-heartedly swat me away, throwing curses at me
with a dusty slipper.

She cursed God. Cursed her callused feet.
Cursed the rains that never stopped.
Cursed the sagging cot. Cursed the sun.
Cursed the flies on the wall.
Cursed the high price of fish. Cursed my mother.
Cursed the iron. Cursed the fat cook
and the lazy houseboy. Cursed her wrinkled face,
her sagging shoulders, the bony, crooked toes.
Cursed her sleepless nights and the piles of dirty laundry
blaming the midday heat, blaming my evil upbringing,
threatening me with blood of the Virgin Mary's womb,
Polynesian gods and Chinese devils.

She promised me that if I was a bad girl,
that if I was a wild and godless child,
naked robbers with greasy skin
would slip into my bedroom
and cut off my sucking thumb with bolo knives.
Roaches and rats with tails as long as typhoons
would steal me from my bed, tie me up, bite out my eyes
and send me in an old suitcase to Borneo.

Still I stood by the door, stayed all day if I could
to watch Pasing push the heavy iron, starch our party dresses,
smoke her cigar and kill horseflies
with bloody slaps of her slipper.

I stayed to hear the curses of her fierce, old tongue,
to learn the swears by heart, shriller—
more savage than I had ever heard
from the mouth of a woman.

I stayed to watch her kill each horsefly
that landed on the cuffs
of my father's white shirts.

*Pronounced *Pa - sing* with the accent on second syllable *sing*. The *a* in Pasing is pronounced like the *a* in *mama*. In the Philippines, a *lavandera* is a woman who does the wash.

■ Cynthia Huntington

Black Cat Waits for Death by the Road

> *The whole of the wideness of night is for you,*
> *A self that touches all edges . . .*
>
> "A Rabbit as King of the Ghosts"
> Wallace Stevens

Crouched here in the grass, in the half dark, the grass humming
because it is high spring, first dawn, warmth rising
from the radiant earth, sending a tremolo of little green
extensions of wave upward in their own lives, to be subject
    to air, I feel

the imperceptible sway in the grasses, taste hunger
in advance of the sun. There is food in the silent house
past here, but first the desired true thing, called to me,
whether mouse or bat, the chipmunk sending a shiver along the
    ground, and

the counterweight stillness of me in the grass, green eyes'
humming attention, the listening in air as I crouch here, death
droning on, the buzz inside the root of things. Attention.
Eight feet beyond, the road gives up its quiet; faster in flight
    the huge engines

burn by, desirable, random firings along a black, charred wire.
Beside the road, a robin's wing pinned down by blue, tilts above
this blur in which I wait. Desirable. My strategy, stillness,
my self, waiting on death by the road: "a self that touches
    all edges."

■ Mark Webster

County Fair

I
Morning By the Ox-Pull Pit

Hair stiff as long-toothed combs
beards sprouting silver
in the peach-skin cast
of early light

we're out of our heads
on rank beer drained
from cups scattered across
the hard turf
beaded with dew

from which dust will soon rise
in masks on sweaty lips
a taste of manure and crushed hay

as we vie to drive piles
with the heavy wood mallet
in a private contest amongst us,
the strongest of men.

II
Ladies' Bazaar

Let the townhouse ladies
approach the grounds
with their handfuls of pies

and cheap cut-glass bowls
to catch the nickel pitches
of boys who hoard coins
with passion that borders
on jealousy.

And let the gaining sun burn
a heartfelt blue
beyond stanchions freshly-wrapped
in spider webs stirred

by hand-painted fans
that brush thin powdered faces
withholding heat, agitation.

III
The Ox-Pull

Quiet comes over the pit
ringed with red-stained snow fence
as a tan-coated team enters
driven by a boy
with a peeled birch switch.

"Sweet mother, make them work,"
his club-toed father growls,
moving up to the clean line

a good bastard who phoned to say
one day last summer,
"wife's dead," settled
the receiver, sent the boy
out to tend the chickens.

Mechanics of beasts interests me;
this team is long-limbed and square.
When the traces are hooked

I wager they'll clean out this pit,
not like has been seen for years.

IV
Last Hour

One last ride on the big wheel
for the weekend girls
of the traveling hands.

Across the grounds
steam rises in languid tails
as the band by the low brick school
plays its swan song.

Couples circle and sway
stepping slowly, sturdy
as seed planters, fence walkers.
Flustered, they kiss.

Beyond in the fields
the stars cluster in view
closing in on a young couple's first kiss.
Tonight, they will learn about composure,

they will lose all regard for rest.

Contributors

Rick Agran's first book of poems was *Crow Milk* (Oyster River Press, 1997). Introduced to the world available in poetry at the University of New Hampshire, he's been published in and co-edited *Aegis* there. Poems have appeared in NH's *Book Love, Compass Rose, Kettle of Fish* and *The Portsmouth Annual.* He hosts *Bon Mot,* a poetry and spoken word radio show on WUNH, Durham, 91.3 FM. Twice nominated Poet Laureate of Portsmouth, he has poems on the CD compilation, *High on Poetry.* He and friends co-founded the City Hall Poets in Portsmouth, NH.

L. R. Berger's work has been supported by the National Endowment for the Arts, the NH State Council on the Arts, the PEN New England Discovery Award and the MacDowell Colony. Her poems have appeared widely in journals and anthologies including *Prairie Schooner, The American Voice, Descant* and *The American Literary Review.*

Lisa Bourbeau has new work forthcoming in *Yankee, First Intensity, Poet Lore* and *Nedge.* A 1997 participant of the Bread Loaf Writers' Conference, Lisa is President of GFS Building Maintenance, Inc. She shares a hilltop in Francestown, NH with her three rescued greyhounds and her "hellhound."

Esther Buffler was born in farmlands of lower Poconos. Breath in act, theatre schooled; early marriage, two sons; children's storyteller, ABC, Austin, TX; published three children's books (one Inter-Americas winner). Widowed, returned NYC, SAG, AFTRA, EQUITY; B'way, Shakespeare Festival; TV, travel, writing. Moved to seacoast. POETRY. Workshops, poet in schools, education, readings; First Poet Laureate, Portsmouth, NH; CD, Library Talk Poetry Series. Into Millennium, aged 90.

W.E. Butts has published poetry in several magazines, and is the author of *Movies in a Small Town* (Mellen Press). A Portsmouth Poet Laureate nominee, and the recipient of a Pushcart nomination, he teaches English and writing at the University of New Hampshire, Hesser College and New Hampshire College.

Colleen Connors celebrated Poetry Month with a workshop for Girl Scout Troop #756 and together they hammered out a poem from a bowl of stones. Her poems appear in *The Denver Quarterly, The South Carolina Review* and *Mudfish.* When not writing poetry on yellow legal pads, she's scribbling it around the edgings of her etchings. Most recently she's trying to find a way to marry poetry to sculpture.

Hildred Crill, a member of the Arts in Education roster at the NH State Council on the Arts, teaches poetry in the schools and at the NH Writers' Project Young Writers' Conference, as well as a poetry workshop for teachers in the Lesley College Creative Arts in Learning program at off-campus locations including Las Vegas, NV and Raymond, NH. Her poems have appeared in two NH-based journals, *The Portsmouth Review* and *Compass Rose.* She lives in Lee, NH.

Mark DeCarteret is the author of *Review—A Book of Poems* (Kettle of Fish Press, 1995). His poetry has appeared in numerous New Hampshire reviews including *Compass Rose, Granite Review, Lungfish Review, The Portsmouth Review, Two Ton Santa* and the anthology *Ad Hoc Monadnock.* A City Hall Poet, he hosts/coordinates poetry readings at Stroudwater Books in Portsmouth, NH.

Stephen Dignazio is a resident of Easton, NH and is co-editor of the poetry magazine *:that:.* His poems have appeared in numerous small press periodicals, chapbooks, and on the web at www.thing.net/~grist/l&d/dignaz.htm, and increasing explore the visible aspect of language (literally writing, its space and materials) as inclusive of, but not limited to, its verbal content. This interest has led to several collaborations with visual artist Evan Haynes, most recently the two person show LIT. at the AVA Gallery in Lebanon, NH and the VI International Biennial of Experimental Poetry in San Diego.

William Doreski teaches creative writing at Keene State (including a poetry workshop every fall), and has published several books of poetry and criticism, mostly recently *Suburban Light* (Cedar Hill, 1999 [poetry]) and *Robert Lowell's Shifting Colors* (Ohio University Press, 1999 [criticism]).

Christopher Dornin has spent most of his thirty-year career as a high school English teacher and as a social worker with prison inmates and people with traumatic head injuries and developmental disabilities. At Williams College he studied creative writing with William Jay Smith. Dornin's poems, published in a dozen journals known only to poets, often deal with the impaired people he has closely served. He never lived in the same cell with the clockmaker in "This Guy I Share My Cell With," but he helped a similar inmate trustee and wood worker to clean up part of the mess after the Christmas Day riot of 1975 at NH State Prison.

James Duffy holds an MFA in Writing from Vermont College. His poems have appeared in *The Aurora, Contemporary Review, the eleventh Muse* and *Ploughshares.* He participated in the 1998 Poetry Jamboree, a poetry reading by New England poets in Portsmouth, NH. He resides in Keene, NH where he works as an investigator for the New Hampshire Public Defender.

Robert Dunn is presently Poet Laureate of Portsmouth, NH, which sounds odd, but Portsmouth is that kind of town.

Rebecca Mays Ernest lives in Dover, NH with her husband, John. Her work has appeared in two chapbooks and in the magazines *Sagetrieb, Tinfish* and *Chain,* among others. The University of New Hampshire and Red's Shoe Barn help with any expenses the cat can't handle.

Patricia Fargnoli of Keene, NH, teaches poetry at The Keene Institute of Music and Related Arts. Pat, who was a 1998 MacDowell Fellow, is an assistant editor of *Victory Park* and *The Worcester Review.* She has been widely published in such journals as: *Poetry, Ploughshares* and *Prairie Schooner.* Her first book, *Necessary Light,* (Utah State University Press,1999) won the 1999 May Swenson Poetry Award.

Alice B. Fogel is the author of *Elemental* and *I Love This Dark World.* Her honors include a fellowship from the NEA. Alice is active as an artist in the schools, and gives writing and other creative arts workshops for all ages. She organizes and raises funds for alternative education and community arts programs.

Jeff Friedman is the author of two collections of poetry, *Scattering the Ashes* and *The Record-Breaking Heat Wave.* His poems have appeared in *American Poetry Review, Poetry, Antioch Review, Manoa, New England Review* and *Press.* A recipient of an Individual Artist Fellowship from the NH State Council on the Arts, he teaches creative writing at Keene State College.

Kate Gleason is the author of *Making As If To Sing* and *The Brighter The Deeper.* Her work has appeared in *Best American Poetry* and *The Los Angeles Times Book Review.* An NEA/Ragdale Fellowship recipient and a state Fellowship Finalist, she teaches writing workshops, was a Poet-in-the-Schools and editor of *Peregrine.*

Francis Golffing, whose first collection of poems was published by Cummington Press in 1950, taught for twenty years at Bennington College, and was dean at Franklin Pierce College. His other books include *Selected Poems* (Macmillan, 1961), *Collected Poems* (University of Nebraska at Omaha, Abattoir Editions, 1980) and *Possibility: an Essay in Utopian Vision* (P. Lang, 1991). He lives in Peterborough, NH.

Donald Hall was born in Connecticut. He published his first book of poems in 1955, and most recently *Without*, about the illness and death of Jane Kenyon. In 1975 he returned to his New Hampshire family farm with Jane Kenyon.

Sidney Hall, Jr. visits and teaches creative writing classes in schools. His poems have appeared in numerous magazines, and his book reviews have appeared in the *Los Angeles Times Book Review*. He is the author of a book of poems, *What We Will Give Each Other*, and a book of memoirs, *Small Town Tales*.

Marie Harris is a poet, editor and freelance writer. She has taught writing workshops and performed her work at schools, universities and libraries throughout the country. She served on the NH State Council on the Arts, first as resident artist, then as Councilor. Her travel articles have appeared in numerous newspapers and magazines. Her poetry is collected in four volumes, the most recent being *Weasel in the Turkey Pen* (Hanging Loose Press) and *Your Sun, Manny* (New Rivers Press).

Alison Harville is a member of City Hall Poets and randomly participates in local poetry readings. A graduate of the University of New Hampshire with a BA in English Teaching, she works with computers for a living. In spare time, she reads, writes, wanders and wonders.

Hugh Hennedy taught reading and writing of poetry for thirty-six years at the University of New England, where he is Professor Emeritus. He has read his own poetry to audiences in New England, California and New York City. His poems have been published in periodicals in this country and in England. His books of poems are *Old Winchester Hill* (Enright House, 1993) and *Halcyon Time* (Oyster River Press, 1993). For the last eighteen years he has lived in Portsmouth, NH.

Robert Herschbach moved to New Hampshire a few years ago to finish a graduate degree and teach. Before that, he attended the Iowa Writer's Workshop, where he received an MFA. He has been a guest on Rick Agran's *Bon Mot.* His chapbook, *A Lost Empire,* was published by Ion Books in 1995, and he's currently completing a book-length manuscript.

Ellen Hersh's poems and translations have appeared in *Bone and Flesh, Ad Hoc Monadnock,* and other reviews and anthologies. Inspiring students of all ages in New England and Florida, Ellen holds degrees from Radcliffe, Yale, and an MFA in Poetry from Vermont College of Norwich University.

Andrew Howe received his BA in English from the University of New Hampshire in 1993, where he won the Richard M. Ford Memorial Award for Fiction and Poetry writing. Currently an active member of the Portsmouth City Hall Poets, he frequents area poetry readings and the local dog park. He lives in Portsmouth, NH.

Cynthia Huntington is the author of two award-winning collections of poetry: *The Fish-Wife* (University of Hawaii Press, 1986), and *We Have Gone to the Beach* (Alice James Books, 1996), as well as a book of prose nonfiction, *The Salt House: A Summer On The Dunes Of Cape Cod* (University Press of New England, 1999). She teaches at Dartmouth College and in the MFA in Writing Program at Vermont College.

Lysa James toured New Hampshire in a production of poetry, storytelling and song entitled *Womenswerk,* which was awarded grants from the NH State Council on the Arts and the Humanities Council. She has read at the Women's State Penitentiary, the University of New Hampshire and many local schools. James's poems have appeared in journals including *Red Brick Review* and *Granite Review.*

Matt Jasper has been too busy chasing babies to come up with a proper or improper bio note but will have his men working around the clock on aforementioned note until such time as it can be telexed.

Hope Jordan is a magazine editor who lives in Canterbury, NH. Her poems have appeared in *Potato Eyes, Caffeine* and *Ad Hoc Monadnock,* among other publications. She's done readings throughout the Merrimack Valley—both solo and with the Yogurt Poets, a Concord, NH-based writing group. A member of the NH Writers' Project, she also won two Boston poetry slams.

J. Kates is a poet and literary translator who lives in Fitzwilliam, NH.

Jane Kenyon was born in Ann Arbor, Michigan, in 1947. In 1972 she left Michigan for New Hampshire, where she lived with her husband

Donald Hall, until she died of leukemia in 1995. Her posthumous new and selected poems, *Otherwise*, appeared in 1996.

Peter Kidd, a native of New Hampshire, makes his living as a landscape design contractor. The publisher of Igneus Press, he is also a poet and novelist.

Maxine Kumin was Poet Laureate of the State of New Hampshire from 1989 to 1994. She received the NH Writers' Project Lifetime Achievement Award in 1998 and the Ruth Lilly Poetry Prize from the Modern Poetry Association in 1999. *Selected Poems 1960-1990* (W.W. Norton, 1997) is her most recent collection. Her memoir, *Inside the Halo and the Journey Beyond* (W. W. Norton), will appear in 2000.

Rodger Martin is a NH State Council on the Arts Touring Artist and member of its Arts in Education roster. He organizes the Monadnock School of Poetry holding readings and monthly workshops at Del Rossi's in Dublin, NH and teaches at the NH Writers' Project Young Writers' Conference. Some New Hampshire credits include *Yankee*, *Granite Review*, *Ad Hoc Monadnock* and *Lungfish Review*.

Cleopatra Mathis is the author of four books of poems, most recently *Guardian*, 1995; all from Sheep Meadow Press in New York. Since 1982, she has taught English at Dartmouth College, where she founded the current creative writing program. She occasionally gives workshops for the elementary and high school students in local schools.

Mekeel McBride's new book, *Zero Gravity*, will appear in 2000 from Carnegie-Mellon University Press. She is putting together a New and Selected Poems that should come out in two or three years. She has eight cats, a dog named Sparky and will be working part time at Happy Wheels in the fall.

Andrew T. McCarter keeps a notebook in New Hampshire. He studied notebookery in school. His job has nothing to do with his notebook, but his notebook has a thing or two to do with his job.

Richard W. Moore lives in Deerfield, NH. He is a member of the Yogurt Poets, who meet monthly at a yogurt shop in Concord, and has participated in readings at the Frost Farm in Derry, Barnes and Noble Bookstore in Manchester, and a slam or two. Aside from an appearance in *A Tray Full of Lab Mice* and a lot of non-fiction articles in defunct regional magazines, most of his publications are in the form of memos and desperate e-mails on behalf of the Audubon Society of New Hampshire, of which he is president.

Donald M. Murray is the author of *Crafting a Life in Essay, Story, Poem* (Boynton/Cook Heinemann, Portsmouth, NH, 1996), among other books. He writes and lives in Durham, NH. The advice attributed to Horace—*nulla dies sine linea*—never a day without a line—is his practice. Well, most days.

Catherine O'Brian grew up in the Philippines and has lived in New Hampshire for the past twenty-five years. A co-founder and contributing editor of *Red Brick Review*, she was runner up for the Grolier Poetry Prize (1993) and in 1995 received the University of New Hampshire's Thomas Williams Graduate Poetry Award for her manuscript, *The White Nightgown.*

Julia Older's verse drama, *Tales of the François Vase*, debuted on NH Public Radio. Engagements have included the *Edith Wharton Lecture Series* with readings from her novel *The Island Queen* and *Celia Thaxter; Selected Writings*. The Smithsonian chose her poem "Summering" to display at the Washington Folklife Festival in 1999.

Pat Parnell, Stratham, NH is co-editor of *Compass Rose*, the journal of art and writing at White Pines College, Chester, NH where she is professor emerita of Communications and Media. "Sheila the Hat" appears in The Poetry Vending Machine and in *Return of the Goddess 1999*, and it has been accepted for publication this year by Shambhala in *Her Words, An Anthology of Poetry about the Great Goddess.* Pat reads "Sheila the Hat" on the CD *High on Poetry.*

Jean Pedrick is the author of *Wolf Moon, Pride & Splendor, Greenfellow* and several chapbooks. Her new book *Catgut* is forthcoming from Salmon Publishing in Ireland. She lives from May to November at Skimmilk Farm in Brentwood, NH, where she holds a peer workshop, ongoing since 1975. She winters in Boston.

Charles W. Pratt, a long-time English teacher at Phillips Exeter Academy, now owns and operates with his wife Apple Annie, a small orchard in Brentwood. Books: *In the Orchard* (Tidal Press, 1986) and *Fables in Two Languages* (self-published as Pomme Press, 1994). Local readings at Phillips Exeter, Water Street Books (Exeter, NH), etc.

James Rioux, a native of New Hampshire, lives in Exeter and participates in a monthly workshop and various readings in the area. His work has been accepted in several New Hampshire publications including *Yankee* and *Color Wheel.*

Mark W. Roberts has been writing and teaching "north of the notch" for fifteen years. In the classroom, he uses poetry to engage, enrich and delight. He lives in Lisbon, NH, just down the road a piece from The Frost Place. His work has appeared in *Magnetic North, Bone and Flesh, Wind* and elsewhere.

Charles Simic is the author of fourteen books of poems. He has lived in New Hampshire since 1973.

Ralph Sneeden's poems from his book-length manuscript—*Off Little Misery Island*—have appeared recently or are forthcoming in *Poetry, The Kenyon Review, Ploughshares, The Southern Review, TriQuarterly, New England Review, Gray's Sporting Journal* and in *The Second Set: The Jazz Anthology of Poetry*, eds. Feinstein/Komunyakaa (Indiana University Press). He lives and teaches at Phillips Exeter Academy, Exeter, NH.

Katherine Solomon teaches at the New Hampshire Technical College in Claremont. Her poems have appeared in *Green Mountains Review, Baybury Review, Victory Park, Compass Rose, Columbia Poetry Review, Worcester Review* and others. Her poem, "Near Firenze," took first prize in the 1998 New England Regional Poetry Contest of the Monadnock Writers' Association.

S. Stephanie is a nurse in Portsmouth, NH. Her work has appeared in many small and literary magazines. She holds an MFA in Poetry from Vermont College. She has conducted poetry workshops for the elderly and children, as well as tutored privately. She co-organized/hosted the Seacoast Repertory Theater's 1998-99 poetry reading series. "Evening Interrupted by Dali" is the title poem of an unpublished manuscript. Her new and forthcoming work can be found in *The Sun* and *The Café Review.*

William Varner's work has appeared in *Green Mountains Review, Mudfish* and *The Greensboro Review*, among others. In recent years, he's taught workshops in the Seacoast area, given a few readings and was the publisher for the ill-fated journal, *The Portsmouth Review.* He currently works as an acquisitions editor at Heinemann Publishers in Portsmouth.

Chris Volpe, a resident of Newmarket, NH, teaches a poetry workshop for undergraduates at the University of New Hampshire, where he earned a master's degree in writing poetry in 1996. He has been featured as a local poet in the *Portsmouth Herald*, and has been a guest on WUNH's *Bon Mot* radio show. He is currently organizing an undergraduate spoken word night at The Red Onion in Durham. His work has appeared most recently in *The New Republic*, *New American Writing*, *The Prose Poem* and *Blink*, a New York City fanzine.

Melanie Walsh is a 1998 graduate of the University of New Hampshire where she received writing awards for her poetry and non-fiction. While attending UNH, Melanie coordinated Live Poets Society and co-edited the literary journal *Aegis*. "inventory" is her first published piece outside of UNH.

James Washington Jr. has participated in several poetry readings and writing workshops for New Hampshire high school students. His poetry has appeared in *The Anthology of New England Writers*, *Journal of Progressive Human Services*, *Lowell Review*, *Pegasus* and *Red Brick Review*. He lives in Durham, NH and is Director of Admissions at the University of New Hampshire.

Mark Webster, born in Hanover, NH, in 1960, received a BA in English from the University of New Hampshire, was a graduate student in poetry at the University of Michigan when he died in 1989. His formative years were spent in the village of Etna, NH, on his family's 200 acre sheep farm. He was profoundly influenced by long hours spent in those woods (running, skiing, writing and exploring with his dog Cinnamon), where he uncovered the wonders of, and perhaps even communed with, the nature around him. He was a competitive swimmer, skier and runner, and before entering graduate school, was an Associate Director at *Newsweek* magazine in New York.

Don Wellman was born in Nashua, NH (1944). He is Professor of Writing and Humanities at Daniel Webster College. For 10 years he edited *O.ARS*, a series of anthologies, exploring topics in postmodern poetics. His most recent book of poems, *Fields*, is available from Light and Dust Books, Kenosha, WI.

Jennifer White lives in Portsmouth, NH and earned her BA in English at the University of New Hampshire. She recently completed her MFA at Emerson College in Boston, where she was the recipient of the Graduate Dean's Award for outstanding work in poetry.

Mimi White, a veteran of the NH artists in the schools program, teaches poetry to young people. In recent years her work has broadened to include residencies at Temple Israel in Portsmouth, several residencies for the elderly, the NH State Prison for Women, and work with young girls and women funded through Clipper Health. She collaborates with artists Sarah Haskell, Marguerite Mathews and

Greg Gathers. Mimi has been selected to participate in the national residency initiative, Artists & Communities: America Creates for the Millennium. Her poems appear in *Poetry*, *Harvard Review*, *West Branch*, *The Seattle Review* and elsewhere.

Jennifer E. Whitten has taught at Hesser College, the University of New Hampshire's Thompson School and Kittery Adult Education. She has also worked with teens in Epping, NH, and with adult conferences on the Seacoast and on Star Island. She considers teaching an honor, and feels blessed in the presence of students who teach even more than they learn.

Andrew Woolf has performed folk music and read his poetry at Northern Essex Community College, Aryaloka and Stroudwater Books.

About the Editors

Rick Agran, now a resident of coastal New Hampshire, grew up in Brookline, NH and was raised (mostly) in the Live Free or Die state. Interested in the intersections between image-making in art and poetry, he teaches writing for Tufts University at the School of the Museum of Fine Arts in Boston, MA. At the New Hampshire Institute of Art he's associate poetry editor of the journal *Victory Park*, and teaches Poetry and Composition. He studied creative writing at the University of New Hampshire, where he received his MA in 1995. Studying Poetry at Sarah Lawrence College, he edited the *Sarah Lawrence Review* and received his MFA there in 1993.

Hildred Crill has worked as a freelance editor and proofreader. Her poems have appeared in *Poetry, Colorado Review, Cream City Review, The Literary Review, Poet Lore* and elsewhere. She was a 1999 recipient of a Ragdale fellowship.

Mark DeCarteret has helped out editing at *AGNI, Emerson Review* and *The Portsmouth Review*. His poetry has appeared in a wide range of journals including *Atlanta Review, Caliban, Chicago Review, Cream City Review, Exquisite Corpse* and *Salt Hill*.

Permissions

We gratefully acknowledge the publications in which the following poems appeared previously. They are reprinted here by permission of the individual poets, who hold the copyrights to their poems.

L.R. Berger: "The Carpenter's Son" appeared in *Convergence.*

Esther Buffler: "Lost Head" from *String of Beads* by Esther Buffler. The Golden Quill Press, Francestown, NH, 1981.

Mark DeCarteret: "Bernadette, the Saint" appeared in *Atlanta Review.*

Stephen Dignazio: "boustrophedon" from *QU AT RA IN* by Stephen Dignazio. Oasis Press, Stephen Ellis, ed., Amman, Jordan, 1997, and on the web, Light & Dust Books, ed. Karl Young.

William Doreski: "September Baptismal" from *Piano in the Woods* by William Doreski. Pygmy Forest Press, Eureka, CA, 1998.

James Duffy: "Prayer" appeared in *the eleventh MUSE.*

Robert Dunn: "In your absence I have written your name" from *quo, Musa, tendis* by Robert Dunn. Peter E. Randall, Portsmouth, NH, 1983.

Patricia Fargnoli: "Watching Light in The Field" appeared in *The Connecticut River Review.*

Jeff Friedman: "J, the Chronicler" from *Scattering the Ashes* by Jeff Friedman. Carnegie Mellon University Press, 1998.

Kate Gleason: "After the Foreclosure Sale" from *The Brighter The Deeper* by Kate Gleason. Embers Press, 1995.

Francis Golffing: "To a Friend Who Found It Difficult to Write" from *Collected Poems* by Francis Golffing. The University of Nebraska at Omaha/Abattoir Editions, 1980.

Sidney Hall, Jr.: "Field Song" from *What We Will Give Each Other* by Sidney Hall, Jr. Hobblebush Books, Brookline, NH, 1993.

Marie Harris: "The Seventh Day," copyright © 1993 by Marie Harris, from *Weasel in the Turkey Pen* by Marie Harris. Hanging Loose Press, Brooklyn, NY.

Alison Harville: "Themes On Distance" appeared in *The Café Review.*

Ellen Hersh: "Sweet Georgia Brown" appeared in *Bone & Flesh #14—Symposium On Song.*

Cynthia Huntington: "Black Cat Waits for Death by the Road" appeared in *Third Coast.*

J. Kates: "Out" appeared in *Mid-American Review,* 1985.

Jane Kenyon and Donald Hall: "Words for a Warrant" appeared in *The Café Review.*

Peter Kidd: "Awaiting the Monster's Phone Call" from *Bear Stew* by Peter Kidd. Igneus Press, Bedford, NH,1996.

Maxine Kumin: "Shelling Jacobs Cattle Beans," copyright © 1986 by Maxine Kumin, from *Selected Poems 1960-1990* by Maxine Kumin. Reprinted by permission of W.W. Norton & Company, Inc.

Rodger Martin: "On the Making of Monica's Poem" appeared in *Bone & Flesh #14—Symposium On Song.*

Donald M. Murray: "December 7, 1997" appeared in *Pivot.*

Catherine O'Brian: "Pasing" appeared in *Red Brick Review.*

Julia Older: "Beached," copyright © 1995 by Julia Older, from *Higher Latitudes* by Julia Older. Appledore Books, Hancock, NH.

Pat Parnell: "Sheila the Hat" appeared in *Return of the Goddess 1999*, copyright © 1998 by Burleigh Muten, ed. Stewart, Tabori, and Chang, New York, NY, 1998.

Charles W. Pratt: "Brass Rubbing" from *In the Orchard* by Charles W. Pratt. The Tidal Press, Cranberry Isles, ME, 1986.

Katherine Solomon: "Hare" appeared in *Green Mountains Review.*

S. Stephanie: "Evening Interrupted by Dali" appeared in *The Aurora.*

Melanie Walsh: "inventory" appeared in *Aegis.*

Mark Webster: "County Fair" from *Along the River Road* by Mark Webster. Paprika Press, Ann Arbor, MI, 1992.

Jennifer White: "A Husband and Wife in the Woods at a Nudist Camp, N.J. 1963: On a Photograph by Diane Arbus" appeared in *The Beloit Poetry Journal.*

Mimi White: "The Quiet" appeared in *Poetry.*

Other Books from Oyster River Press

Along the Roads of the Universe—Por los caminos del universo. Poems by Amor Halperin, author and illustrator, with translations by Ida Halperin. 1997.

Crow Milk. Poems by Rick Agran. 1997.

Edged in Light. Poems by Jane Jordan. 1993.

Halcyon Time. Poems on the birds by Hugh Hennedy. Illustrated by Charles Chu. 1993.

Intense Experience: Social Psychology through Poetry. Fred Samuels, Editor. 31 poems with commentaries, an index of concepts, an essay on Erickson's theory of the Eight Ages of Man by James Halla. 1990.

Is it Poison Ivy? A field guide to Poison Ivy, Oak and Sumac and their look-alikes. 2nd ed. Joan Raysor Darlington. 1999.

A Letter to my Daughter by the Marquis of Halifax, 1687 (George Sevile) with *Essays from a New England College Town, 1926-1987* by Phoebe Taylor.

The Mending of the Sky and other Chinese Myths. Translations from the classical Chinese by Xiao Ming Li. Illus. Shan Ming Wu. 1989.

Peace in Exile. Poems by David Oates. 1992

Shadows & Sun~Ombres et Soleil. Writings of 1913-1952 by Paul Eluard. Illus. by Picasso, Magritte, Chagall and Andre Lhote. Translations by Cicely Buckley & Lloyd Alexander. 1995

Thoughts for the Free Life: Lao Tsu to the present. Cicely Buckley, Editor and Illustrator. Lao Tsu, Sophocles, Schweitzer, Cervantes, Neruda, Native Americans, Thoreau, etc. from 5 continents, 25 centuries. Illustrated. 3rd ed. 1997.